MAZE
QUEST
GEOGRAPHY

How to use this book

Have you packed your passport and your toothbrush? Then you're ready to join George and Milly on an amazing geography quest across the globe!

The big picture . . .

Geography is all about places and people around the world. In this book you'll visit many locations as you complete each maze. On the left-hand pages, read fascinating facts and stats about each maze destination. Learn about famous cities, awesome landmarks and beautiful landscapes and habitats. And follow George and Milly's adventures at each destination.

Paris, France

Enjoy a stroll along the River Seine and take in the sights and smells of Paris, the capital of France. The French are famous for their food and their smelly cheeses are some of the best in the world. George is pleased as he's hungry for a cheese sandwich! See if you can spot the following as George makes his way towards the cheese shop:

Notre Dame Cathedral

The Pyramid at the Louvre Museum

The Arc de Triomphe

The Eiffel Tower

* The French flag is red, white and blue.
* The Louvre Museum houses the painting of the *Mona Lisa* and is the most visited museum in the world.
* The Eiffel Tower is 320 m tall and was the tallest structure in the world from 1889 to 1930.

Kyoto, Japan

After the modernity of Seoul in South Korea, George and Milly experience the traditional side of Japan by visiting Kyoto. Tranquil Buddhist temples, charming gardens and colourful Shinto shrines showcase ancient Japanese culture at its best. After a lunch of sushi, our friends tour the city taking photos of:

The Tō-ji 'East Temple'

The Kinkaku-ji 'Golden Pavilion'

Nijō Castle

The Shimogamo Shrine

* The original name of Kyoto was Heian-kyō, or 'Capital of Peace'.
* There are over 2,000 temples and shrines in Kyoto.
* Every shrine has a red or orange torii gate at the entrance, marking the entrance to the sacred space.

Keep an eye out for the things to spot on the mazes. Make sure you pass each of them listed on the left-hand pages as you follow the routes of the mazes. Why not check them off as you locate them to help you find the correct routes?

Solving the Mazes

George and Milly travel around the world in planes, trains, a hot-air balloon, on an elephant and much more! To get through each maze, find the mode of transport from the end of the last maze. This is your start point! Now make your way through the maze to the exit with the next mode of transport on.

Top tip

Always
follow the main
path – and
look for the
shortest route!

It's time to get started, so turn the page to begin your maze quest. Meet your companions George and Milly, and help George pick up all his luggage from his home. Then the rest is up to you. Good luck and see you at the final destination!

This way...

Are you
ready to
begin your
maze quest?

The Adventure Begins

George is about to set out on the journey of a lifetime! He's off on an adventure around the world. But first he needs to pick up his bag, find his passport and actually leave the house. Can you help him? Find the route from George's bedroom to the front door, and collect these:

 Backpack

 Passport

 Camera

 His pet dog Milly

* George is a Geography teacher who loves discovering new places. He can't wait to start his grand adventure.

* Milly is George's faithful companion. She wonders if all dogs speak the same language.

* George likes cheese sandwiches and Milly enjoys chasing cats!

START

Take To The Skies!

George and Milly arrive at the airport by taxi. It's one big maze! Passengers are flying around the world from this busy airport, and it's open 24 hours a day, every day of the week. Can you spot the following as George and Milly walk towards the departure gate?

A pilot

A sleeping traveller

A large piece of luggage

A lost passport

* The world's busiest airport is in Atlanta, Georgia, USA.
* The largest passenger plane in the world is the Airbus A380-800 and it can carry over 519 passengers, plus crew.
* The longest non-stop flight is from Dallas, USA to Sydney, Australia and takes almost 17 hours.

London, UK

London is the capital city of England, UK, and Queen Elizabeth II lives here at Buckingham Palace. There's so much to do in this big city, including galleries, museums, theatres and restaurants — George and Milly better hop on a red London bus and get moving! See if you can help them spot London's famous landmarks along the way:

Big Ben

The London Eye

St Paul's Cathedral

Tower Bridge

* London is located around the River Thames.
* It has a population of 9 million people.
* Big Ben, at the Houses of Parliament, is the name of the bell inside the tower, not the clock or tower itself!

Paris, France

Enjoy a stroll along the River Seine and take in the sights and smells of Paris, the capital of France. The French are famous for their food and their smelly cheeses are some of the best in the world. George is pleased, as he's hungry for a cheese sandwich! See if you can spot the following as George makes his way towards the cheese shop:

Notre Dame Cathedral

The Pyramid at the Louvre Museum

The Arc de Triomphe

The Eiffel Tower

* The French flag is red, white and blue.
* The Louvre Museum houses the painting of the *Mona Lisa* and is the most-visited museum in the world.
* The Eiffel Tower is 320 m tall and was the tallest structure in the world from 1889 to 1930.

Barcelona, Spain

George is enjoying walking around this city full of art while Milly plays on the beach. Watch out for Antoni Gaudí's amazing gothic cathedral with the four spires, The Sagrada Familia. Take a stroll down the city's beautiful streets and see if you can spot the following street performers:

A juggler

A caricaturist

A string quartet

A unicyclist

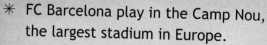

* FC Barcelona play in the Camp Nou, the largest stadium in Europe.
* The Sagrada Familia is the most visited monument in Spain.
* The city of Barcelona has seven beaches to enjoy.

Venice, Italy

The floating city of Venice is made up of 118 small islands linked by bridges. George and Milly board a gondola and are taken on a tour around the canals. Their guide points out the top sights — just make sure you pass them:

St Mark's Basilica

A person eating an ice cream

Doge's Palace

The Rialto Bridge

* Venice is sinking into the water at a rate of 1-2 mm a year.
* It has over 170 canals and over 400 bridges.
* The narrowest street in Venice is only 53 cm wide!

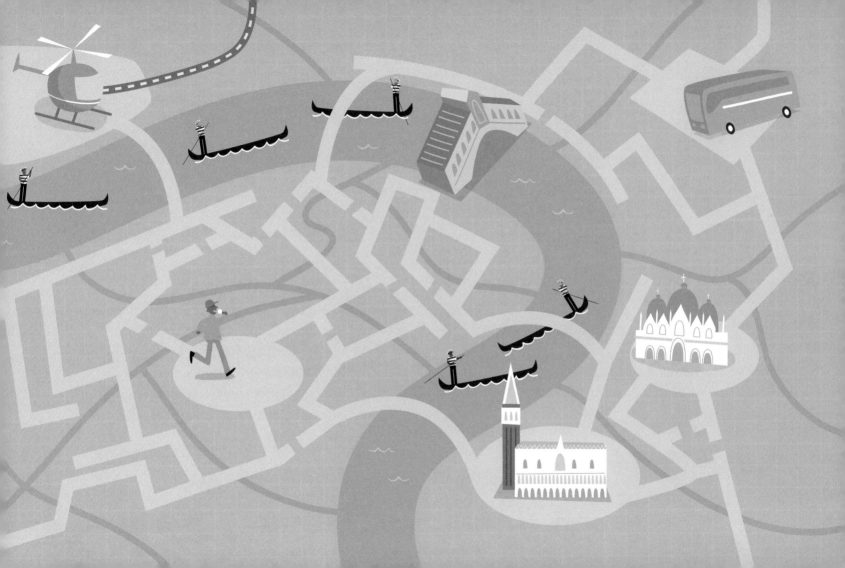

The Swiss Alps, Switzerland

George and Milly arrive in the alpine region of Switzerland. This is an area of mountains over 2,000 m above sea level. Milly wants to race to the top of Monte Rosa, the highest peak, but George is more excited about trying the hot chocolate at one of the alpine lodges! See if you can spot the following:

 The skier with the red hat

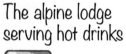 The alpine lodge serving hot drinks

 A lost rambler

 Buttercups

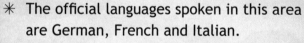

* The official languages spoken in this area are German, French and Italian.
* Monte Rosa is 4,634 m high.
* The Aletsch glacier is the largest glacier in the Swiss Alps. A glacier is a body of moving ice.

Berlin, Germany

Berlin is the capital of Germany and its largest city. It was bombed heavily during World War II, but is now a centre for culture, art and business and has a wide variety of architecture. George decides to get on a city tour bus and passes these famous sights:

Art on the Berlin Wall

The Reichstag

The Brandenburg Gate

The Fernsehturm TV tower

* The river Spree runs through the city centre.
* 'Museum Island' is the name given to a small island with famous museums on it.
* Berlin has around 1,700 bridges — many more than Venice!

Copenhagen, Denmark

Welcome to Copenhagen! George and Milly have travelled here by tandem and are in good company as everyone is cycling here! They head straight to Tivoli Gardens in the centre of the city to experience this famous entertainment park with rides, games, gardens and shows.

 A carousel

 A rollercoaster

 Food stalls

 A pagoda

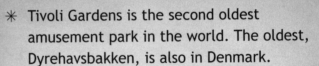

* Tivoli Gardens is the second oldest amusement park in the world. The oldest, Dyrehavsbakken, is also in Denmark.
* Hans Christian Andersen lived in Copenhagen and wrote many of his fairy tales here.
* Copenhagen often tops charts of the best places to live in the world.

Stockholm's Skärgård, Sweden

Sweden is famous for its natural beauty, and George and Milly decide to head into the skärgård (archipelago) around Stockholm for a kayaking trip. Look out for vast pine trees and lakes, the 17th-century Nynäs Manor House and of course all the wildlife:

 A moose

A beaver

 A bat

A wolf

* Stockholm is the capital of Sweden.
* Forests cover over 50 per cent of Sweden and there are around 100,000 lakes.
* The Swedish currency is called krona.

The Northern Lights, Finland

George and Milly are in the very north of Finland watching the beautiful Northern Lights. This is a dazzling display of light in the sky that occurs when charged particles from the sun's solar wind react with Earth's magnetic field. The colours are caused by gases in the air. Milly can't believe her eyes! See if your eyes are working and spot:

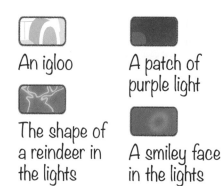

An igloo

A patch of purple light

The shape of a reindeer in the lights

A smiley face in the lights

* Oxygen causes a green or brownish-red display of lights. Helium produces blue or purple colours and nitrogen causes blue or red colours.
* The official name for the Northern Lights is 'aurora borealis'.
* The lights appear on more than 200 nights a year in northern Finland.

Kraków, Poland

Our travellers arrive in the centre of Kraków's old town — the market square. This European city is a UNESCO World Heritage Site and there are around 6,000 historic sites to visit. George and Milly don't have time to visit them all but they do want to see:

The Market Square

Wawel Castle

The Barbican

St Mary's Basilica

* There is a legend that the name Kraków came from a ruler called Krakus, who built the town above the cave of a dragon.
* Kraków was the capital of Poland from 1038 to 1596.
* Central Kraków has a population of less than 1 million, but over 9 million people visit the city each year.

Prague, Czech Republic

Prague is one of the largest cities in central Europe and has a beautiful medieval centre. George and Milly are here in time for the Christmas markets, and the sights and smells create a winter wonderland! George is excited to browse the stalls for traditional handicrafts while Milly is drawn to the local cats! See if you pass the following stalls:

A jewellery stall

A wooden toy stall

A candle stall

A pastry stall

* Prague's most famous Christmas market can be found in the Old Town Square.
* People in the Czech Republic celebrate Christmas on the 24th and 25th December.
* The Christmas tree is traditionally taken from the mountains in the north of the Czech Republic.

Dubrovnik, Croatia

Dubrovnik's walled old town on the Adriatic Sea is a maze of cobbled streets. George and Milly walk the city walls but then need to find their way out via the Pile Gate. Can you help them? You'll need to pass these:

Boys jumping off the wall into the sea

A group of tourists on a guided tour

The clock tower

St John's fortress

* Dubrovnik is often called 'the pearl of the Adriatic'.
* No cars are allowed in the old town.
* The city walls are approximately 2 km in length.

Budapest, Hungary

Help George and Milly navigate their way to the Szechenyi Baths in Budapest. There are three outdoor pools filled with natural hot spring water and everyone is welcome to take a dip. Can you spot the following on the way?

Men playing chess

The Royal Palace

A boy floating like a starfish

St Stephen's Basilica

* The river flowing through the city is the Danube.
* The water in the Szechenyi Baths has a temperature of up to 38°C.
* Hungarian is a unique language and has no significant similarities to any other language in the world.

Greek Islands, Greece

"Time for some relaxation," says George, and he and Milly jump on a boat from Athens and head out into the Aegean Sea. There are so many islands to explore and Milly loves swimming in the clear blue water. In the distance they can see the Acropolis, the remains of an ancient Greek settlement above Athens, but in the sea they spot:

A red
sailing boat

Olive trees on
an island

Dolphins

A person waterskiing
off the back of a boat

* There are over 6,000 Greek islands.
* Only 227 of the islands are inhabited.
* The largest Greek island is Crete.

Istanbul, Turkey

Istanbul is a transcontinental city – half of it is in Europe and the other half is in Asia. It's surrounded by seven hills, each with a mosque on the top. George and Milly join a city tour to see the sights and pass:

The Grand Bazaar

Hagia Sophia

Topkapi Palace

The Blue Mosque

* Istanbul has been the capital of three major empires: Roman, Byzantine and Ottoman, but it is not the capital of Turkey.
* The city only got the name Istanbul in 1930, before that it was called Constantinople.
* In the time of the Ottoman Empire the city boasted around 1,400 public toilets. Other European cities at this time had none!

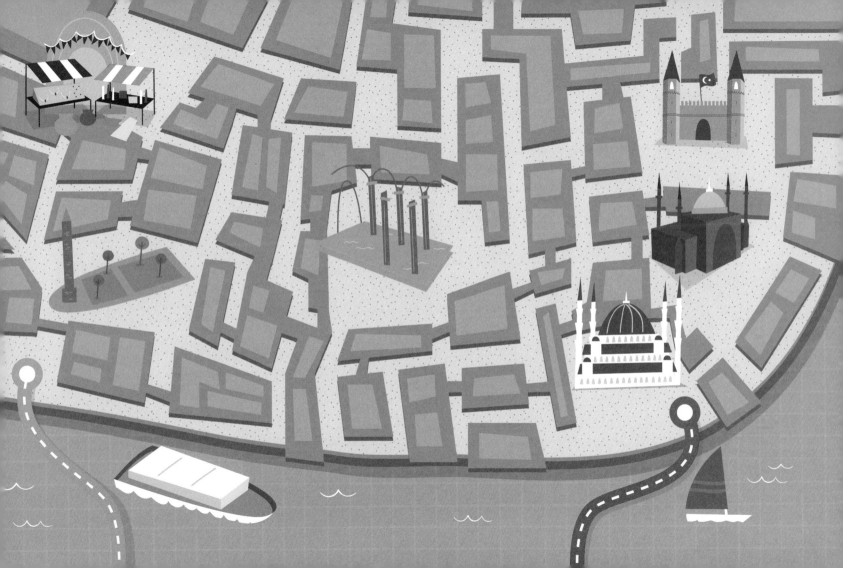

The Great Pyramid of Giza, Egypt

George and Milly enter Africa by visiting Egypt. Any visit here has to include a trip to see the Great Pyramid of Giza, the only ancient wonder of the world that still exists today. Inside the pyramid is a maze of passages with three burial chambers. It's believed the pyramid was built as a tomb, so make sure our friends don't get lost looking for:

Treasure

A lost tourist

A pharaoh's mask

Hieroglyphics (ancient script)

* It's thought that the Great Pyramid was originally 146.5 m tall, but due to erosion it's now only 138.8 m high.
* It's made of an estimated 2.3 million blocks.
* It's believed the pyramid was built for Egyptian pharaoh Khufu around 2570 BC.

Marrakesh, Morocco

The souks — or markets — of Marrakesh are alive with people, noise and smells. Goods have been traded here for hundreds of years — including gold and leather. Nowadays tourists still visit to find pretty gold jewellery or a new leather bag, but it's also fun to walk around and get lost in the maze of alleyways! Can you help George find:

A carpet for his home

A new leather collar for Milly

Some spices to cook with

A gold necklace for his mother

* Sweet mint tea is a popular drink in Morocco made with fresh mint leaves.
* Couscous is a popular traditional dish containing tiny granules of durum wheat.
* Marrakesh is located between the Atlas Mountains and the Sahara Desert.

Safari, Kenya

Kenya has some of Africa's top wildlife and a safari is the best way to see lions, elephants, leopards, wildebeest, and much more. George and Milly venture out into the Maasai Mara National Park with their guide, Naomi. Look out for the following animals:

The lion cub

An elephant having a wash

Two leopards having a race

Birds on the back of a wildebeest

* The Maasai Mara National Park covers an area of 1,510 sq km.
* The migration of wildebeest across the Maasai Mara to Tanzania is one of the great natural wonders of the world.
* The Maasai Mara has one of the largest populations of lions in the world.

Victoria Falls, Zambia

Get as close to this gigantic waterfall as you can,
without actually being in the water! It's lucky George
and Milly remembered to pack their rain jackets. As they gaze
through the mist at the waterfall, see if you can help them spot:

A rainbow

A crocodile

A log shaped
like a car

A canoeist at the
top paddling away
from the falls

* The falls are on the Zambezi river,
  the fourth longest river in Africa.
* The falls were named after Queen Victoria
  by David Livingstone in 1855, but the
  indigenous name of 'Mosi-oa-Tunya' is
  also used.
* It has the highest volume of water of any
  waterfall in the world.

Tsingy de Bemaraha Nature Reserve, Madagascar

This national park is a UNESCO World Heritage Site and is famous for its wildlife as well as its limestone rocks that look like needles coming out of the ground. Lemurs are native only to Madagascar and Milly can't wait to meet the locals. See if you can spot:

The lemur eating leaves

The lemur jumping out of a tree

The lemur asleep in a tree

The lemurs grooming each other

* There are thought to be around 100 living species, and subspecies, of lemur.
* The smallest lemur is the pygmy mouse lemur.
* The largest lemurs are the indri and sifaka species, which are about the size of a cat.

The Burj Khalifa, Dubai

From a natural wonder to a man-made wonder – George and Milly arrive in Dubai and can't miss the world's tallest building! They decide to take the lift to the top rather than climb the stairs, and get a fantastic view of Dubai, the most populous emirate in the United Arab Emirates. There's lots going on in the Burj Khalifa:

A party in a hotel room

A person asleep on an exercise bike

A waiter dropping a tray of drinks

A bird on the very top of the building

* At over 828 m high the Burj Khalifa is the tallest building in the world.
* It has over 160 floors.
* It has 24,348 windows.

The Taj Mahal, India

India has what is believed by many to be the most beautiful building in the world – the Taj Mahal. The central Taj structure is made of white marble with a central dome surrounded by four minarets (spires). George and Milly are speechless as they walk around this astonishing structure with its ornamental gardens, and when they've finished their tour they realize the building is symmetrical. Can you help them spot:

The lotus pond

Patterns in the marble walls

Yamuna river

Agra Fort

* The Taj was completed in 1653 by Emperor Shah Jahan.
* It was built as a final resting place for Mumtaz Mahal, the third wife of Emperor Shah Jahan.
* It is said to have taken around 20,000 people to build it.

The Great Wall of China, China

George and Milly are visiting the Great Wall of China – the longest structure ever built by humans. The Great Wall was built over many years to protect China's northern boundaries. According to legend, a helpful dragon traced out the course of the Great Wall for workers to follow. Watchtowers appear at regular intervals and were used as lookouts. See if you can spot:

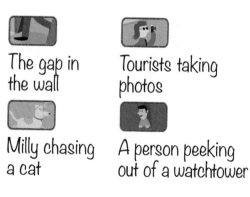

The gap in the wall

Tourists taking photos

Milly chasing a cat

A person peeking out of a watchtower

* It's hard to tell exactly how long the Great Wall is, but it's thought to be over 21,190 km long.
* It was built over a period of 2,000 years.
* The highest point of the Wall is around 8 m tall and the widest point is around 9 m wide.

Beijing, China

George and Milly don't have far to travel from the Great Wall of China to China's capital city, Beijing. They arrive during Chinese New Year, a period of festivities to mark the start of the lunar calendar. They watch a colourful dragon dance — a traditional part of the celebrations believed to chase away bad luck.
See if you can spot:

A dragon with 8 humps

A dragon with a gold head

A dragon with a red tail

A lion

* Red is the most prominent colour during Chinese New Year — it symbolizes fortune, good luck and joy.
* Each year is named after an animal on a 12 year cycle. The animals are: rat, ox, tiger, rabbit, dragon, snake, horse, ram, monkey, rooster, dog and pig.

Moscow, Russia

The city of Moscow is known for its unique architecture and George immediately spots St Basil's Cathedral with its colourful domes. This city is also the centre of the Russian Government, and the Kremlin is a fortified complex that houses the government and the president's home. Can you find these four iconic places in the city?

The Kremlin

Red Square

The Bolshoi Theatre

St Basil's Cathedral

* Moscow is named after the river that runs through it, the Moskva.
* Moscow has a population of over 12 million people.
* The Russian currency is called the ruble.

Seoul, South Korea

This busy city is active day and night and George and Milly are dazzled by the bright lights as they view the city from the top of the N Seoul Tower. The city is buzzing with technology and George uses a tablet device to help him locate these Seoul landmarks:

Gyeongbok Palace

Dongdaemun Design Plaza

Seoul City Hall

The moonlight rainbow fountain at Banpo Bridge

* The N Seoul Tower rises 479.7 m above sea level.
* The trains on Seoul's subway have heated seats!
* Seoul has served as a royal capital since 1394.

Kyoto, Japan

After the modernity of Seoul in South Korea, George and Milly experience the traditional side of Japan by visiting Kyoto. Tranquil Buddhist temples, charming gardens and colourful Shinto shrines showcase ancient Japanese culture at its best. After a lunch of sushi, our friends tour the city taking photos of:

The To-ji
'East Temple'

The Kinkaku-ji
'Golden Pavilion'

 Nijō Castle

 The Shimogamo Shrine

* The original name of Kyoto was Heian-kyō, or 'Capital of Peace'.
* There are over 2,000 temples and shrines in Kyoto.
* Every shrine has a red or orange torii gate at the entrance, marking the entrance to the sacred space.

Ha Long Bay, Vietnam

Ha Long Bay in the north of Vietnam means 'Bay of the Descending Dragons' and legend has it that the islands were formed from jewels dropped from the mouth of a dragon. George and Milly cruise around the bay and take in its beauty. Milly takes the opportunity to go for a swim! See if you can spot:

Jumping fish

A boy jumping off a boat

The shop in the floating village

The 'kissing rocks'

* There are around 1,600 tall, rocky limestone islands in Ha Long Bay.
* Many of the islands have names based on their shape e.g. 'elephant rock', 'human face' and the 'kissing rocks'.
* There are many caves in Ha Long Bay as the water erodes the soft limestone rocks.

Angkor Wat, Cambodia

Angkor Wat is a group of temples in Cambodia. It is a religious monument for the Buddhist faith and was built in the 12th century. Milly runs off to explore the passageways of the temple and George is left to try and find her. Can you help him get to Milly by passing:

Buddhist monks

The carving on the wall

The smiling statue

The tree roots growing over a doorway

* Angkor Wat appears on Cambodia's national flag.
* It is the largest religious monument in the world.
* The name translates as 'city of temples'.

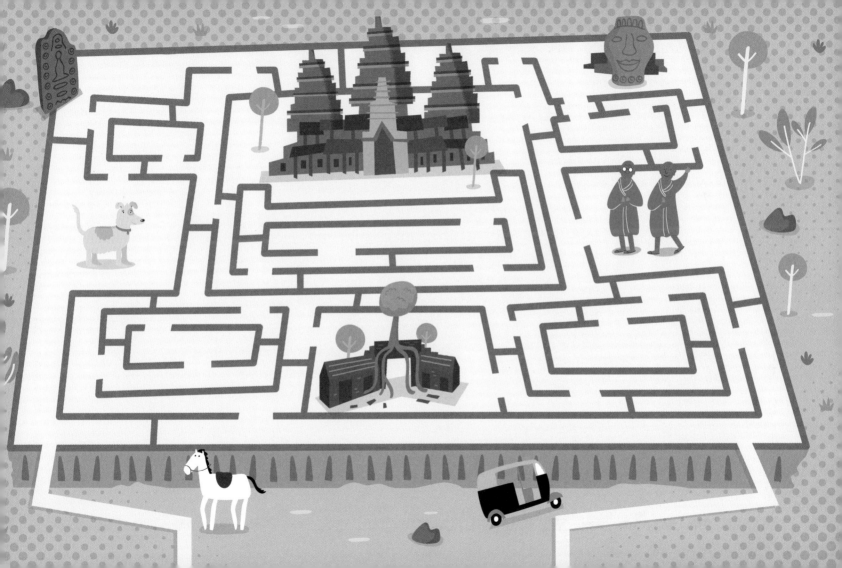

Phuket, Thailand

George and Milly are excited to learn how to scuba dive in Thailand! They join a group on the island of Phuket and their instructor takes them offshore and underwater. It's another world down here, and the fish are all the colours of the rainbow. Can you spot:

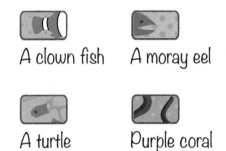

A clown fish   A moray eel

A turtle   Purple coral

* The island of Phuket is in the Andaman Sea.
* Phuket is Thailand's largest island.
* SCUBA diving stands for Self-Contained Underwater Breathing Apparatus.

Kuala Lumpur, Malaysia

Kuala Lumpur, KL, is a capital city with an interesting mix of old and new — historical monuments, mosques and temples sit next to modern skyscrapers and shopping malls. The most famous landmark is the Petronas Towers, twin towers that look like rockets. George and Milly head to the top to get a view of the city, but can you spot them and these other people?

An excited baby

George and Milly

A window cleaner

An office worker at her desk

* The towers are 88 storeys high and were officially opened in 1999.
* The towers' floor plan is based on an eight-sided star.
* They are the world's tallest twin towers.

Sydney, Australia

Sydney Harbour provides a glamorous entrance to Australia for George and Milly. They get a birds-eye view of this stunning natural harbour as they fly over it in a biplane. The city revolves around the water and there are over 100 harbours and ocean beaches to enjoy, as well as world-class food, culture and sport. George points out Sydney's top attractions to Milly from the air:

The Opera House

Taronga Zoo

The Harbour Bridge

The Botanical Gardens

* The Harbour Bridge is known as the 'coat hanger' by locals due to its distinctive shape.
* Danish architect Jørn Utzon won a competition to design the Opera House in 1957.
* Sydney was first settled on 26th January 1788. The 26th January is celebrated as 'Australia Day'.

Queenstown, New Zealand

Welcome to the adventure capital of New Zealand! This town on the south island of New Zealand is situated on the edge of Lake Wakatipu and surrounded by The Remarkables mountain range. If you want an adrenaline rush you can sky dive, bungee jump, white water raft, canyon swing and more! Milly wants to try them all so make sure she passes:

The bungee jump bridge

The white water rapids

The snowy mountain edge

The speed boats on Lake Wakatipu

* The oldest person to bungee jump at the Kawarau Bridge Bungy was 94.
* Queenstown offers over 220 adventure tourism activities.
* The area around Queenstown was used for many scenes in *The Lord Of The Rings* film trilogy.

Suva, Fiji

"Bula!" "Hello!" and welcome to Fiji. George and Milly have arrived in a country that represents island paradise and a day of snorkelling, sailing and relaxing on the beaches awaits. They decide to hop on a boat and visit the Mamanuca Islands and Yasawa Islands. On route they pass:

A blue lagoon

Coral reefs

Manta rays

The Sawa-I-Lau caves

* Fiji is made up of 322 islands.
* The capital city is Suva on the island of Viti Levu.
* Fiji was a British colony until 1970 when it gained independence.

Hawaii, USA

Hawaii is the 50th State of the USA and the only one located in Oceania. It is the birthplace of 'big wave' surfing on the island of Oahu, and George and Milly arrive on competition day. The competitors all try to catch the biggest wave and surf it to the shore. Just watch out for sharks in the water! Can you spot?

The surfer in the air

The surfer falling off his board

The surfer with a pink board

The surfer being chased by a shoal of fish

* Surfing is known as 'he'e nalu' in Hawaiian.
* Surfing is believed to have originated in Polynesia.
* The biggest waves ever surfed are around 24 m high.

New York, USA

New York, nicknamed the 'Big Apple', is the most populated city in the United States and has a buzzing centre on the island of Manhattan. On this small strip of land are hundreds of world-famous sights that George has seen in movies. A good place to view them is from the top of the Empire State Building on Fifth Avenue. George points out these locations to Milly:

The Statue of Liberty

Central Park

The Empire State Building

The Brooklyn Bridge

* Around 800 different languages are spoken in New York, making it the most linguistically diverse city in the world.
* The New York Subway system is the largest in the world according to number of stations — 468 in total.

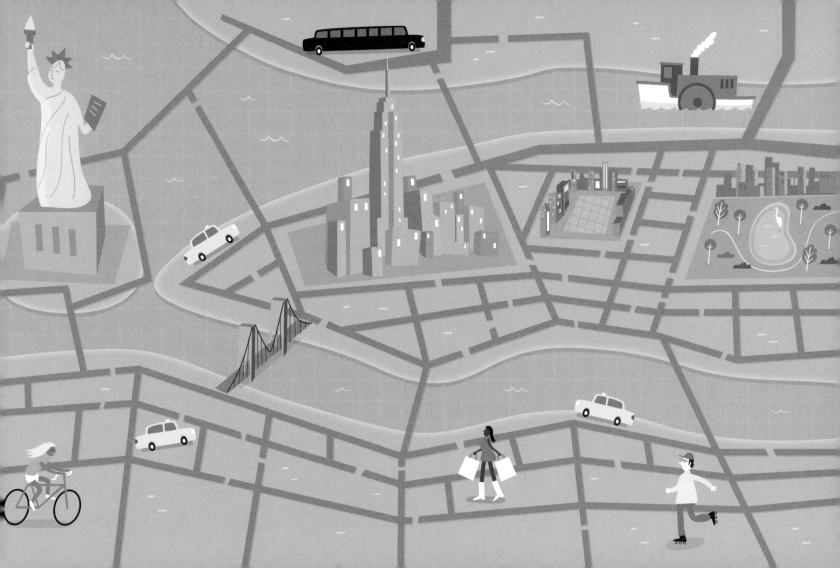

Popocatépetl, Mexico

Mexico lies on the 'ring of fire', an area around the Pacific Ocean where lots of volcanic eruptions and earthquakes occur. Popocatépetl is an active volcano 70 km southeast of Mexico City and it has had more than 15 major eruptions since 1519. George and Milly join a hike to climb to the top, and hope it doesn't erupt today! Help them follow the path by passing:

A Mexican volcano rabbit

An ash cloud shaped like an aeroplane

A bird peering into the volcano

Cooling lava

* Popocatépetl is a stratovolcano — a conical volcano built up of layers of hardened lava.
* It is 5,426 m high.
* According to studies the volcano is about 730,000 years old.

The Amazon rainforest, Colombia

Thirty-five per cent of Colombia is covered by the Amazon rainforest, and George and Milly are exploring it.
The rainforest consists of four layers: the emergent layer at the top with the tallest trees and lots of birds; the canopy layer with dense trees for animals like monkeys to explore; the understorey with shrubs, insects and reptiles; and the forest floor where more insects and mammals roam. Spot these animals hiding in the trees:

 A capuchin monkey

 A red-eyed tree frog

 A jaguar

 A toucan

* One in ten of all known species in the world live in the Amazon rainforest.
* The forest is spread across nine nations in South America.
* The rainforest covers 5,500,000 sq km.

The Blue Mountains, Jamaica

The small island of Jamaica is famous for the coffee grown in its Blue Mountains. George is invited to help harvest some coffee seeds. He has to pick the berries from the coffee plants, dry them out and then remove the seeds. The seeds are then roasted and ground before being brewed to create the drink. George enjoys his hot coffee in the shade of the mountains and he observes:

 The smallest coffee tree

 The tree with the most coffee berries

 The bags of beans

The person with the largest mug of coffee

* Blue Mountain Peak is 2,256 m above sea level.
* The Blue Mountains are so named because the mists and lush vegetation give the area a greenish blue tinge.
* Coffee is the second-most-traded commodity in the world, after oil.

Machu Picchu, Peru

George and Milly arrive in Peru and embark on a trek to the lost Inca city of Machu Picchu. It's the best-known archaeological site in the whole of South America, and is around 2,430 m above sea level. The city was split into three areas — agricultural, urban and religious — and may have been a site for sacred ceremonies. Our friends start the tour from the steps of Intihuatana hill and look for:

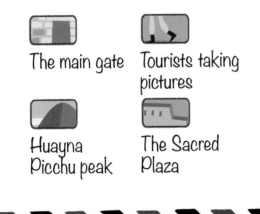

The main gate   Tourists taking pictures

Huayna Picchu peak   The Sacred Plaza

* Machu Picchu was built around 1450, at the height of the Inca Empire.
* The site was unknown outside of Peru until 1911 when an American historian discovered it.
* Only 400 visitors per day are allowed into the site.

Rio de Janeiro, Brazil

Welcome to the Rio Carnival! The streets of this magnificent city are filled with samba dancers and lively musicians to celebrate this yearly festival. The samba schools competing against each other are in the Sambadrome, each hoping to be crowned this year's champion. Milly is in the party spirit and is dancing on Copacabana Beach. Can you see what George is doing? He might be at one of these spots:

Ipanema Beach

The Sambadrome

Sugarloaf Mountain

Christ the Redeemer Statue

* The Rio Carnival marks the start of Lent, the forty-day period before Easter.
* Samba is a Brazilian dance with African origins. It's also the name of the music.
* There are over 200 different Samba Schools in Rio de Janeiro.

Buenos Aires, Argentina

George and Milly have made it to Buenos Aires, the capital of Argentina. This city has a European look to it but a Latin American vibe. The city is full of famous landmarks, including the area of La Boca with its colourful houses. Make sure George and Milly pass:

The Obelisk

The Teatro Colon opera house

The Casa Rosada – president's mansion

La Bombonera – Boca Juniors' football stadium

* Buenos Aires has the highest concentration of theatres in the world.
* People of Buenos Aires are referred to as 'portenos' — people of the port.
* Buenos Aires has the widest street in the world — it's 16 lanes wide!

Antarctica

The bottom of planet Earth is like no other place. This frozen continent is not permanently inhabited by humans, which has left it free for wildlife to take charge. The temperature in winter averages between -10 and -30 °C so George and Milly have wrapped up warm. They ask a local scientist to name some of the animals they see:

An elephant seal

A wandering albatross

A blue whale

Emperor penguin chicks

✳ Around 98 per cent of continental Antarctica is covered in ice up to 4.7 km thick.
✳ The coldest temperature ever recorded on Earth was -89.2°C at the Vostok station in 1983.
✳ In winter it is dark for almost 24 hours a day in Antarctica.

The Rocky Mountains, Canada

The Canadian Rockies are a mountain range in western Canada and provide the perfect backdrop for George and Milly to hike, camp and fish in the national parks. To find a place to camp, they jump in an open Canadian canoe and paddle downstream. On the way they spot lots of wildlife including:

A grizzly bear   A bald eagle

Canada geese   A moose

* There are five national parks located in the Canadian Rockies — Jasper, Banff, Waterton, Kootenay and Yoho.
* Mount Robson is the highest peak in the Canadian Rockies at 3,954 m high.
* The Rocky Mountains extend all the way to New Mexico in the southwestern United States.

Haukadalur Geothermal Area, Iceland

Iceland is a geologically active island with volcanoes, glaciers, fjords and geysers. George and Milly visit the geothermal area of Haukadalur and the Strokkur Geyser that erupts every 5-10 minutes, shooting a jet of water up to 40 m into the air. Look out for:

Bubbling mud pools

Hot springs

Strokkur Geyser

Steaming fumaroles

* Geysers form when surface water runs down into the ground and comes into contact with rocks heated by magma. The water boils and the pressure forces it to erupt in a jet.
* There are over 1,000 geysers worldwide.

Home, Sweet Home

After visiting over 40 countries George and Milly decide it's time to head home. They travel in style for the last leg of their journey on a cruise ship. The ship is a floating hotel with a pool, many restaurants, a theatre and a gym, but George and Milly have seen so many incredible sights on their journey that all they want to do is sit down, look at their souvenirs and remember their great adventure. Can you identify the countries these objects have come from?

An Eiffel Tower keyring

A cuddly toy giraffe

A coffee cup

A snorkel and mask

* George and Milly visited a total of 17 countries in Europe.
* They made two stops in both China and the USA.
* They've used 47 different vehicles and modes of transport to travel around the world.

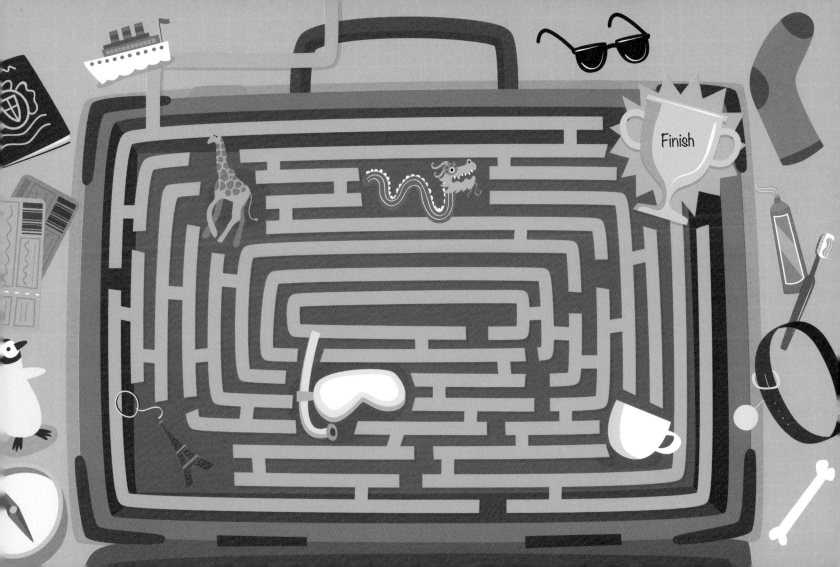

Finish

The Answers

1. The Adventure Begins

2. Take To The Skies!

Shhhh!... TOP SECRET!

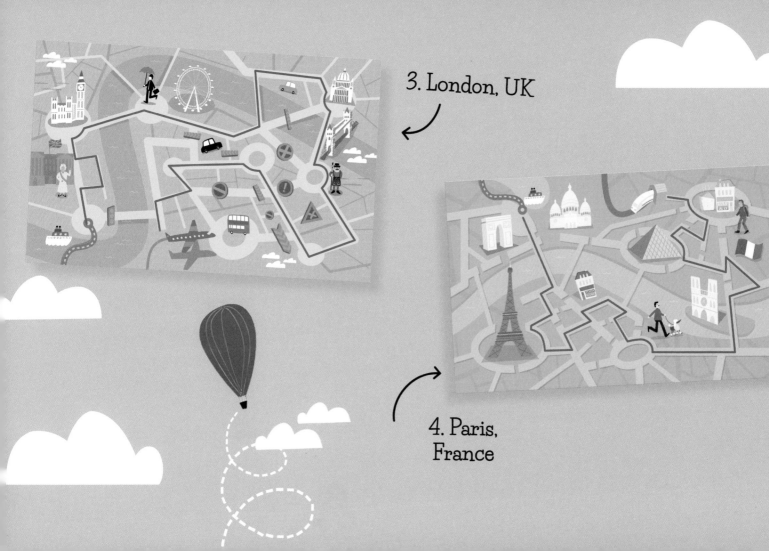

3. London, UK

4. Paris,
France

5. Barcelona, Spain

6. Venice, Italy

7. The Swiss Alps, Switzerland

8. Berlin, Germany

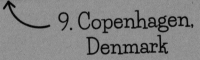

9. Copenhagen, Denmark

10. Stockholm's
Skärgård,
Sweden

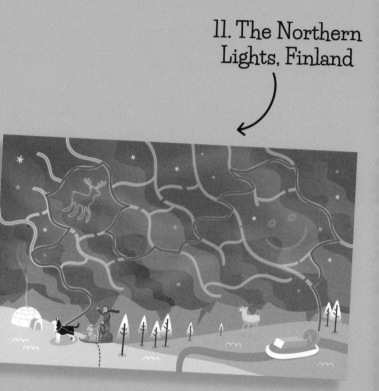

11. The Northern
Lights, Finland

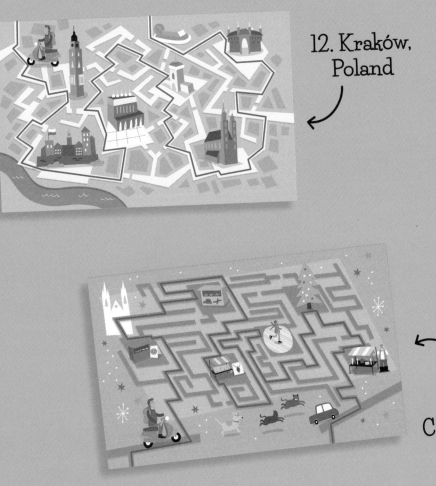

12. Kraków,
Poland

13. Prague,
Czech Republic

14. Dubrovnik,
Croatia

15. Budapest,
Hungary

16. Greek Islands,
Greece

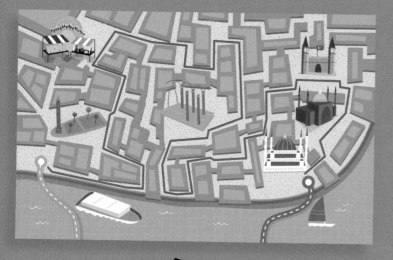

17. Istanbul,
Turkey

18. The Great
Pyramid
of Giza, Egypt

19. Marrakesh,
Morocco

20. Safari, Kenya

21. Victoria Falls,
Zambia

22. Tsingy de Bemaraha
Nature Reserve,
Madagascar

23. The Burj Khalifa, Dubai

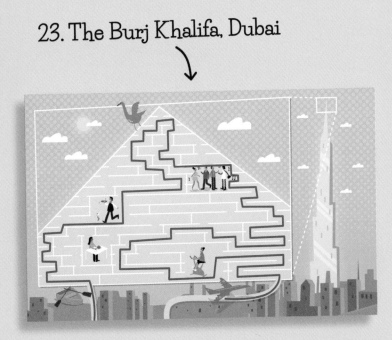

24. The Taj Mahal, India

25. The Great Wall
of China, China

26. Beijing, China

27. Moscow,
Russia

28. Seoul,
South Korea

29. Kyoto, Japan

30. Ha Long Bay, Vietnam

31. Angkor Wat,
Cambodia

32. Phuket, Thailand

33. Kuala Lumpur, Malaysia

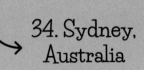

34. Sydney, Australia

35. Queenstown,
New Zealand

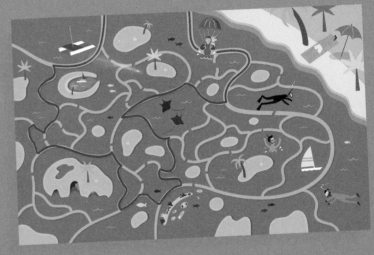

36. Suva, Fiji

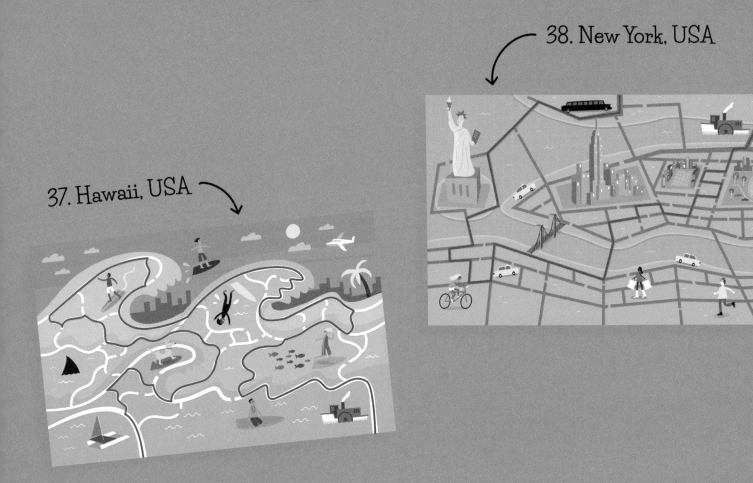

37. Hawaii, USA

38. New York, USA

39. Popocatépetl,
Mexico

40. The Amazon
rainforest, Colombia

41. The Blue Mountains, Jamaica

42. Machu Picchu, Peru

43. Rio de Janeiro, Brazil

44. Buenos Aires,
Argentina

45. Antarctica

46. The Rocky
Mountains, Canada

47. Haukadalur
Geothermal Area, Iceland

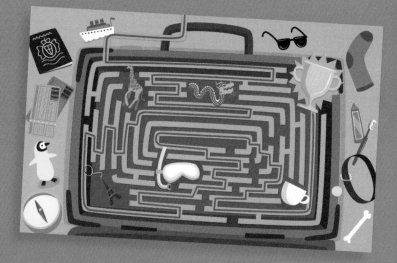

48. Home, Sweet Home